About the Author

An esteemed expert in cybersecurity, the author leverages their distinguished military background in Communications and IT to offer unparalleled insights into the digital security landscape. With over two decades of intensive experience, they have honed their skills in developing and implementing robust cybersecurity measures tailored to protect organizations against an array of evolving threats. Their unique blend of military discipline and industry know-how sets them apart as a thought leader in this increasingly critical field.

Throughout their career, the author has engaged with a multitude of high-profile organizations, including local and central government departments across the UK. This extensive professional background has not only enriched their technical prowess but has also equipped them with real-world experiences that inform their writing. Their hands-on approach ensures that they stay attuned to the latest trends and challenges in cybersecurity, making them a credible voice in advocating for better safety strategies in the digital age.

Educationally, the author boasts a solid foundation that amplifies their authority on the subject of cybersecurity. Influenced by both formal education and practical application, their journey as a writer was spurred by a desire to demystify complex cybersecurity concepts for a broader audience. The decision to pen "Cyber Security: Dark Side of AI" is rooted in their commitment to enhancing public understanding of the pressing security issues we face today, particularly in an era where artificial intelligence intertwines increasingly with our lives.

In addition to their technical skills, the author's ability to communicate intricate ideas with clarity and relatability makes their writing engaging and accessible. They strive to make cybersecurity less daunting and more relatable, breaking down complex topics so that readers from all backgrounds can grasp the essentials. Their passion for teaching is evident in their interactive approach, as they often share personal anecdotes and real-world examples to foster a deeper understanding of key issues and solutions.

The author's mission is to illuminate the critical importance of cybersecurity in our digital world, aiming to equip organizations and individuals with the knowledge they need to protect themselves in an ever-evolving landscape. Looking ahead, they aspire to continue sharing their insights through writing, speaking engagements, and consulting opportunities, paving the way for a safer digital future for everyone. Their goal is not just to inform but to inspire proactive measures that safeguard our interconnected lives.

Table of Contents

Chapter 1: Introduction to AI in Cyber Security

(3) - 1.3 Objectives of the Book

Chapter 2: The Architecture of AI Systems

Chapter 3: Understanding Threat Intelligence

Chapter 4: AI in Network Security

Chapter 5: Machine Learning Algorithms in Cyber Security

Chapter 6: The Dark Side of AI

Chapter 7: Ethical Considerations in AI Deployment

(1) - 7.1 Ethical Dilemmas in Cyber Security

(2) - 7.2 Bias and Fairness in AI Algorithms

(3) - 7.3 Regulatory Compliance for AI in Cyber Security

Chapter 8: AI for Incident Response

(1) - 8.1 Automating Incident Detection

(2) - 8.2 AI in Incident Analysis and Recovery

(3) - 8.3 Lessons Learned and Continuous Improvement

Chapter 9: Future Trends in AI and Cyber Security

(1) - 9.1 Evolution of AI Technologies

(2) - 9.2 Predicting Future Threat Landscapes

(3) - 9.3 Preparing for Emerging Technologies

Chapter 10: Building a Security Architecture with AI

(1) - 10.1 Defining Security Architecture Principles

(2) - 10.2 Frameworks for Incorporating AI

(3) - 10.3 Best Practices for AI Implementation

Chapter 11: Risk Management and AI

Chapter 12: Securing AI Systems

Chapter 13: Collaboration between Cyber Security and AI

(1) - 13.1 Interdisciplinary Approaches

(2) - 13.2 Sharing Insights between Domains

(3) - 13.3 Leveraging AI in Cyber Security Teams

Chapter 14: Training and Skill Development

Chapter 15: Conclusion and Future Outlook

(1) - 15.1 Summarizing Key Insights

(2) - 15.2 Future Challenges and Opportunities

(3) - 15.3 Final Thoughts on AI in Cyber Security

Chapter 1: Introduction to AI in Cyber Security

1.1 Overview of AI Concepts

Artificial Intelligence (AI) is a multidisciplinary field that simulates human intelligence through machines, enabling them to perform tasks that normally require human cognition. Its core components include machine learning, deep learning, and natural language processing. Machine learning focuses on algorithms that allow computers to learn from and make predictions based on data without being explicitly programmed for specific tasks. Deep learning, a subset of machine learning, involves neural networks with many layers that process vast amounts of data in ways that mimic human thought processing. Natural language processing (NLP) enables machines to understand, interpret, and respond to human language, bridging the gap between human communication and machine understanding.

The evolution of AI technologies began with foundational theories in symbol manipulation and has advanced through the application of statistical methods to enormous datasets. This evolution has led to significant improvements in various sectors, particularly in addressing contemporary challenges within cybersecurity. As cyber threats become increasingly sophisticated, AI technologies offer powerful solutions for identifying patterns, detecting anomalies, and responding to threats in real-time. Cybersecurity professionals are leveraging AI to enhance their threat detection capabilities and automate responses to security incidents, thereby improving the resilience of network architectures and planning.

Understanding and effectively integrating AI into cybersecurity frameworks can significantly enhance an organization's security posture. For instance, AI can be programmed to analyze network traffic patterns and quickly identify deviations that may indicate a breach. By employing AI-driven tools, security architects can bolster defenses against evolving threats, ensuring that their systems not only react to incidents but also learn from them to pre-emptively defend against future attacks. Prioritizing the integration of AI technologies in cybersecurity planning is vital for maintaining robust defenses in an ever-changing digital landscape.

1.2 Importance of AI in Cyber Security

AI significantly enhances traditional security measures by introducing advanced capabilities in threat detection and response. Traditionally, security systems relied heavily on defined rules and manual monitoring, which often resulted in delayed responses to emerging threats. AI addresses these limitations by employing machine learning algorithms that can analyze vast amounts of data in real time. These algorithms learn from historical data, recognizing patterns and anomalies that could indicate potential cyber threats. This proactive approach allows organizations to identify threats before they escalate into serious breaches. By using AI, security frameworks can automate routine tasks, such as log analysis and vulnerability scanning, freeing human experts to focus on more complex security challenges that require nuanced decision-making. The ability to respond to threats quickly and efficiently is critical in a landscape where cybercriminals are becoming increasingly sophisticated and agile.

Examining real-world case studies highlights the effectiveness of AI in mitigating cyber threats. For instance, a major financial institution integrated AI-driven solutions into its cybersecurity strategy, resulting in a significant decrease in detected intrusions. By utilizing AI technologies for behavioural analytics, the institution was able to monitor user activity and identify deviations from normal behaviours. Suspicious activities triggered automatic alerts, enabling swift investigation and response. Another case involved a healthcare provider using AI to enhance its network security. The AI system managed to identify ransomware attacks in their infancy by correlating data from numerous sources and enabling early intervention. These examples demonstrate how blending human expertise with AI-powered tools can transform cybersecurity operations, making them more resilient and adaptive to evolving threats.

For cybersecurity professionals, understanding when and how to incorporate AI into network planning and architecture is crucial. It is important to assess the specific needs of the organization, including the types of data processed and the potential risk landscape. Selecting AI tools that align with the organization's goals and existing systems can provide enhanced security coverage. Organizations should also prioritize training and developing internal capabilities for personnel to work effectively with AI technologies. Regularly updating AI systems and algorithms based on the latest threat intelligence ensures that they remain effective against emerging threats. Involving stakeholders in the implementation process can foster a culture of security awareness and readiness to adapt to new technologies.

1.3 Objectives of the Book

This book aims to explore the intersection of artificial intelligence and cyber security, addressing how these technologies can synergize to enhance network planning, architecture, and security strategies. Each chapter will delve into key themes such as the capabilities of AI in identifying vulnerabilities, automating responses to incidents, and improving threat intelligence. Readers will find discussions on machine learning algorithms and their applications in anomaly detection, predictive analysis, and behaviour modeling, all crucial for advanced security infrastructures. By the end of this exploration, cyber security professionals can expect a thorough understanding of the benefits and challenges associated with integrating AI tools into their existing frameworks.

Establishing a solid framework for understanding the application of AI in cyber security involves contextualizing its use alongside traditional security measures. In a landscape where threats are becoming more sophisticated, AI introduces innovative methods for ensuring system integrity and data protection. The book will unravel case studies demonstrating real-world implementations of AI in network defenses, as well as illustrate scenarios where AI's predictive capabilities can significantly reduce reaction times to threats. This contextual approach will empower cyber security architects and engineers to not only grasp the technical aspects of AI but also appreciate its strategic implications for future-proofing their organizations against evolving cyber threats.

As you engage with the content, consider how your own security environments can benefit from AI deployment. Keeping abreast of the latest tools and techniques in AI can provide a significant competitive edge, enabling you to stay ahead of potential threats. Experimentation with AI applications in your current projects might reveal valuable insights and underscore the importance of continuous learning and adaptation in the ever-changing field of cyber security.

Chapter 2: The Architecture of AI Systems

2.1 Components of AI Systems

The primary components of an AI system consist of data inputs, algorithms, and output mechanisms, each of which plays a crucial role in the functionality and effectiveness of the system. Data inputs are the raw information fed into the AI system, which can include structured data, such as logs, and unstructured data, such as text from social media or network traffic descriptions. This data serves as the foundation for the system's learning and decision-making process. The algorithms are what transform this data into actionable insights. These algorithms can be based on machine learning techniques, deep learning methods, or other statistical methods that enable the AI to recognize patterns, make predictions, and classify information. Output mechanisms then interpret the results generated by the algorithms and relay this information back to users or other systems in a usable format, whether that be alerts, reports, or direct actions that can enhance security measures.

These components work synergistically to facilitate intelligent decision-making in cybersecurity. For instance, an AI system analyzing network traffic relies on vast amounts of data inputs to detect anomalies that could indicate a potential cyber threat. The algorithms assess this data, learning from historical attack patterns and adapting to new threats in real-time. As the AI processes incoming data, it may flag unusual behaviour, triggering alerts through the output mechanisms that inform security personnel about potential risks. This prompt response capacity allows organizations to address threats swiftly, reducing the window of exposure to attacks. An effective AI system, therefore, not only enhances the ability to respond to threats but also improves preventive measures by continually learning from the data it acquires, evolving its understanding of the cybersecurity landscape over time.

By understanding these components and their interplay, cybersecurity professionals can better leverage AI tools in their network planning and security architecture. Adopting a system that can learn from new data and previous incidents will significantly improve threat detection and response capabilities, making it vital for architects and engineers to consider these AI components in their cybersecurity strategies.

2.2 Deployment Models for Cyber Security

The deployment models for artificial intelligence (AI) significantly impact the security architecture of organizations. Two primary deployment models are cloud-based and on-premises solutions. Cloud-based AI applications leverage scalable resources provided by cloud service providers. This model offers flexibility, allowing organizations to deploy systems quickly and adjust capacity based on demand. Security measures, such as data encryption and access controls, are typically core components of these platforms, which are continuously updated to address emerging threats. In contrast, on-premises deployment entails utilizing hardware and software solutions within an organization's own infrastructure. This model provides greater control over data security and compliance, as sensitive information remains within the organization's reach. Organizations can tailor security measures to their specific needs, ensuring improved oversight of their systems. However, on-premises solutions require significant upfront investment and ongoing maintenance, which can strain internal resources.

When evaluating the pros and cons of these models regarding risk mitigation specific to AI applications, the differences become even more apparent. The cloud-based model excels in scalability and rapid deployment, which are vital for organizations needing to pivot quickly in response to cyber threats. However, it also raises concerns about data privacy and dependence on third-party security measures. If the service provider suffers a breach, client data may be compromised as well. On the other hand, on-premises models offer enhanced control and could align better with stringent regulatory requirements concerning sensitive data. Nonetheless, they come with the burden of managing security updates and patches. Additionally, organizations may face limitations in utilizing the latest AI advancements due to constrained resources and expertise. Balancing these factors becomes crucial in determining the most effective deployment model for AI applications.

Understanding the intricacies of deployment models enables cyber security professionals to strategically plan their AI implementations. It is essential to align the chosen model with organizational goals, resource availability, and compliance requirements. When contemplating the deployment of AI solutions, consider the sensitivity of the data involved and the potential impact of security breaches on the organization. Establishing a clear understanding of the threat landscape, combined with an analysis of the deployment environment, can aid in making an informed decision that enhances overall security posture.

2.3 Integration with Existing Infrastructure

Integrating AI systems within current security frameworks requires a systematic approach that aligns the capabilities of AI with the existing technologies and protocols already in place. One effective strategy is to start with a thorough assessment of the current security infrastructure. This involves identifying gaps in the existing system where AI can provide significant enhancements, such as real-time data analysis, threat intelligence, or automation of repetitive tasks. By focusing on areas where AI can complement or augment existing tools, organizations can create a more resilient security posture. Collaboration among cross-functional teams is crucial during this stage, as it ensures that the technical aspects of AI integration are aligned with business needs and security requirements.

However, the integration process does not come without its challenges. One major hurdle is the compatibility of AI systems with legacy technologies. Many organizations rely on older systems that may not be compatible with modern AI solutions, leading to potential disruptions. To tackle this, organizations can explore the use of middleware that enables communication between the old and new systems, facilitating a smoother integration pathway. Another challenge is the need for clean, structured data for AI models to train effectively. Organizations should implement robust data management practices, ensuring data quality and accessibility. Addressing concerns around data privacy and security during the integration of AI is also essential, given the sensitive nature of cybersecurity information. Therefore, establishing clear data governance policies that comply with regulations is a critical step in the integration process.

As organizations navigate through these challenges, a practical tip is to pilot AI solutions in a controlled environment before full-scale implementation. This approach allows teams to monitor performance, assess potential issues, and adjust strategies accordingly. By learning from pilot implementations, organizations can refine their integration processes, ultimately leading to a more seamless transition into an AI-enhanced security framework.

Chapter 3: Understanding Threat Intelligence

3.1 Sources of Threat Intelligence

Organizations today can leverage a variety of sources for threat intelligence, which play a crucial role in enhancing their security posture. Open-source threat intelligence is widely accessible and can be obtained from various public platforms, forums, blogs, and social media channels. The benefit of open-source data is its cost-effectiveness and the broad spectrum of information it provides. However, the major challenge lies in the validation of such information; while it may surface useful insights, the unverified nature often makes it a double-edged sword. To complement this, commercial threat intelligence services offer curated, summarized, and often validated feeds tailored to business needs. These services typically come with various levels of detail, such as incident reports, vulnerability assessments, and threat actor profiles, making them attractive for organizations wanting in-depth analysis and timely updates. Proprietary data, often generated in-house, serves as another critical source. This data offers unique insights drawn from internal network activities and security events, though it requires robust collection mechanisms and analysis capabilities to maximize its potential.

When analyzing the reliability and relevance of these sources concerning real-time security measures, it's essential to consider the context in which the intelligence will be applied. Open-source intelligence may provide timely alerts about emerging threats but lacks the rigor of validation that commercial sources typically uphold. The immediacy of information in open-source channels means it can reflect trends rapidly, making it valuable for situational awareness, but organizations must exercise caution before acting on it. Conversely, commercial sources, while often data-rich and reliable, may sometimes lag in real-time updates due to their structured processing methods. They excel in historical context and actionable insights derived from patterns but may not capture the most transient threats. Proprietary data stands out in this analysis, as it aligns closely with the organization's unique threat landscape, allowing for tailored responses. However, its effectiveness is directly proportional to the quality of the detection tools and skills employed, making continuous investment in personnel and technology imperative.

To optimize the efficacy of threat intelligence, organizations should create a hybrid approach that integrates these diverse sources while employing robust validation mechanisms. Combining insights from open-source, commercial, and proprietary channels not only enhances situational awareness but also allows for a comprehensive defense strategy. In practice, this means utilizing open-source data for initial threat identification, leveraging commercial services for deeper analysis and contextual understanding, and applying proprietary data for fine-tuning detection and response efforts. Regularly assessing and adjusting these sources in relation to the evolving cyber threat landscape will enable organizations to stay one step ahead of potential adversaries.

3.2 AI-enhanced Threat Detection

Artificial intelligence (AI) is transforming how organizations identify anomalies and potential threats within their networks. Traditional threat detection methods often rely on predefined rules and signature-based systems, which can fall short in the face of evolving cyber threats. AI models, on the other hand, can analyze vast amounts of data and learn from patterns, enabling them to detect suspicious behaviour that may not fit known signatures. By leveraging techniques such as supervised and unsupervised learning, AI can differentiate between normal and abnormal activities, offering a more dynamic approach to threat detection. This adaptability is crucial in an environment where cyber adversaries continuously refine their tactics.

To enhance automated threat detection, several specific algorithms and techniques are utilized. One prominent method is anomaly detection, which involves training algorithms on large datasets to establish a baseline of normal behaviour. When behaviour deviates from this baseline, the AI system flags it as a potential threat. Techniques like decision trees, support vector machines, and neural networks are widely employed in crafting these models. Additionally, deep learning approaches, such as recurrent neural networks (RNNs) and convolutional neural networks (CNNs), provide the ability to process complex data streams and identify threats in real-time. These methods not only increase efficiency but also empower security professionals with actionable insights, allowing for a proactive defense posture.

Incorporating AI into threat detection systems presents exciting opportunities for cyber security professionals. It is essential to recognize that while AI can significantly enhance detection capabilities, it should complement existing security frameworks rather than replace them. Organizations may find it beneficial to implement a hybrid approach, where AI systems work alongside traditional security measures. This dual strategy can strengthen overall defenses and ensure that professionals maintain a keen understanding of the evolving threat landscape. Engaging with experts in AI and security can provide valuable insights into tailoring solutions that fit specific organizational needs, thereby maximizing the effectiveness of AI-enhanced threat detection.

3.3 Analyzing Threat Patterns with AI

Artificial Intelligence has transformed the way cyber security professionals analyze vast amounts of data to identify emerging threat patterns. The sheer volume of data generated by network activities, user behaviour, and system logs can overwhelm traditional methods of analysis. AI technologies, particularly machine learning algorithms, can sift through this data at incredible speeds, discovering hidden correlations and anomalies that may indicate the presence of a threat. By leveraging AI, security teams can detect patterns that would otherwise go unnoticed, such as subtle shifts in user behaviour or unusual communications between systems. This capability is especially crucial in today's fast-paced environment where cyber threats evolve rapidly and can lead to devastating consequences.

Once AI has processed and identified potential threats within the data, the next critical step is to visualize and interpret the results. Visualization tools play a vital role in helping cyber security experts translate complex data outputs into understandable formats. For instance, dashboards with graphical representations can highlight areas of concern, enabling professionals to quickly grasp the status of network security. Heat maps may show concentrations of suspicious activities across different segments of a network, while time-series analyses can illustrate trends over time. Moreover, these visual tools can facilitate collaborative discussions among teams, ensuring that insights derived from AI-driven analyses translate into actionable strategies. It's essential for security professionals to choose the right visualization methods that not only communicate findings clearly but also support rapid decision-making processes in an ever-changing threat landscape.

Understanding how to apply AI effectively in threat pattern analysis is crucial for cyber security architecture and planning. To maximize its potential, security teams should continually refine their algorithms and incorporate feedback from on-the-ground experiences. This iterative approach not only enhances the accuracy of threat detection but also builds a proactive defense posture against emerging cyber risks. Staying ahead in this dynamic field requires not only leveraging technology but also ensuring that team knowledge and skills evolve alongside innovations in AI.

Chapter 4: AI in Network Security

4.1 Firewall and Intrusion Detection Systems

Integrating artificial intelligence into traditional firewall and intrusion detection systems (IDS) is revolutionizing the way organizations protect their networks. By leveraging AI, these security mechanisms can analyze vast amounts of data in real time, identifying patterns and anomalies that would be nearly impossible for human analysts to detect swiftly. AI models can be trained on historical attack data to recognize the signatures of various threats, enabling them to adapt as new threats emerge. This dynamic approach allows firewalls and IDS to go beyond just blocking specific traffic and instead assess potential risks based on behavioural trends and context, enhancing their effectiveness significantly. For instance, machine learning algorithms can continuously learn from ongoing network traffic, improving their accuracy over time and reducing false positives, which can burden security teams with unnecessary alerts.

However, while AI-driven firewall solutions offer significant benefits, they also come with limitations that must be acknowledged. One notable advantage is the ability to respond to threats in real time, adjusting configurations and rules dynamically without the need for manual intervention. This agility allows organizations to maintain a robust defense posture even as the threat landscape evolves. In contrast, traditional static rule-based firewalls often struggle to keep pace with sophisticated attacks since they rely on pre-defined rules that can become outdated easily. On the other hand, AI systems require substantial amounts of data to operate effectively, necessitating a strong foundation in data collection and analysis. There is also the risk of adversarial attacks on AI models themselves, where cybercriminals could exploit weaknesses in the algorithms or training data, making it imperative for organizations to remain vigilant and continuously refine their AI systems.

Understanding the interplay between AI-enhanced firewalls and traditional systems is crucial for cybersecurity professionals tasked with network planning and architecture. It is advisable to adopt a hybrid approach that combines the strengths of both methodologies. By integrating AI into the security framework while maintaining a foundational level of static rules, organizations can enjoy the best of both worlds—immediate threat response capabilities complemented by established practices that provide a safety net against the unknowns of evolving cyber threats. Regular training and updating of AI models, alongside an evaluation of the contextual relevance of static rules, will help ensure that the security posture remains robust and resilient over time. Prioritizing continuous professional development in AI technologies for cybersecurity teams can foster an environment of adaptability and informed decision-making in the face of emerging threats.

4.2 AI-Driven Anomaly Detection

Anomaly detection in network behaviour has evolved significantly with the integration of artificial intelligence. Traditional methods often relied on predefined thresholds and rules, which could easily lead to false positives or negatives in the context of sophisticated cyber threats. AI-driven anomaly detection, on the other hand, leverages machine learning algorithms to continually learn from data. These systems analyze vast amounts of network activity to establish a baseline of normal behaviour, accounting for variances caused by legitimate changes in user activity, device configurations, or other factors. By employing techniques such as supervised learning, unsupervised learning, and reinforcement learning, AI can not only identify deviations from this baseline but can also adapt over time to new patterns of behaviour, making it an ideal candidate for modern security challenges.

Real-world applications of AI-driven anomaly detection in cybersecurity highlight its effectiveness in protecting valuable assets within various organizations. For instance, financial institutions have successfully utilized AI to monitor transaction patterns, enabling the rapid detection of fraudulent activities. These systems analyze transaction data in real-time, flagging anomalies that differ significantly from normal behaviour, allowing for immediate investigation and intervention. Similarly, cloud service providers often implement AI-driven tools to monitor user behaviour and network traffic, identifying unauthorized access attempts and potential data breaches. The technology has proven advantageous in environments like critical infrastructure, where even minor deviations can indicate major threats to operational integrity.

Implementing AI-driven anomaly detection requires not only the right technology but also a strategic mindset in terms of integration into existing security frameworks. It is essential for cyber security professionals to prioritize the continuous training of AI models with up-to-date data to ensure accuracy and reliability. Encouraging collaboration between data scientists and security analysts can further enhance the effectiveness of these systems, as domain expertise is crucial for tuning the algorithms and interpreting their outputs. By adopting this holistic approach, organizations can leverage AI not just as a tool for detection, but as a proactive component of their security architecture.

4.3 Adaptive Security Policies using AI

Artificial Intelligence (AI) plays a pivotal role in enhancing the adaptability of security policies within organizations. By leveraging AI-driven analytics, security systems can dynamically adjust policies in response to real-time threat landscapes and behavioural patterns observed across the network. Traditional fixed security measures often fall short in adequately addressing rapidly evolving threats, particularly as cybercriminals refine their tactics and techniques. AI addresses this challenge by constantly analyzing vast amounts of data to identify anomalies, discern patterns, and predict potential vulnerabilities. When a threat is detected, AI systems can implement immediate changes to security protocols, ensuring that defenses are aligned with current risk levels and allowing organizations to respond to attacks with heightened agility and precision.

The implications of adaptive security policies extend far beyond mere threat response. Continuous adaptation fosters a proactive security posture, enabling organizations to manage their security environment more effectively. By integrating adaptive security measures, security teams can focus more on strategic initiatives rather than solely on daily operational tasks. Automated adjustments allow for a seamless flow of security management, which can lead to improved compliance with regulatory requirements and reduced risk exposure. Moreover, as security policies become more responsive to evolving threats, organizations can also benefit from enhanced collaboration between cybersecurity professionals and AI systems. This partnership empowers teams to not only defend against present threats but also to anticipate and mitigate future risks, ultimately transforming the approach to security management.

For cybersecurity professionals looking to implement AI within their security frameworks, it is crucial to prioritize developing systems that can ingest and process a variety of data inputs—from user behaviour to environmental changes. The more diverse the data sources, the better equipped the AI can be in making informed adjustments. Regular training and updating of AI algorithms ensure that they remain effective as new threats emerge, while ongoing evaluation of the adaptive strategies enables organizations to refine their approaches based on real-world performance. Emphasizing adaptability can significantly enhance an organization's resilience against cyber threats, allowing it to stay one step ahead in today's complex and ever-shifting security landscape.

Chapter 5: Machine Learning Algorithms in Cyber Security

5.1 Types of Machine Learning Models

Various machine learning models exist that can significantly enhance cybersecurity strategies, primarily falling into two categories: supervised and unsupervised learning. Supervised learning involves training a model on a labelled dataset, where the input data is paired with the correct output. This model learns the relationship between the input and output and can then predict outcomes for new, unseen data. Typical applications include intrusion detection systems that classify network traffic as either benign or malicious based on historical data. Conversely, unsupervised learning models operate on unlabelled data, identifying hidden patterns or groupings without any predefined classifications. These models are valuable in anomaly detection, where they can signal unusual behaviour in network traffic that may indicate emerging threats.

Each type of model shines in specific contexts. Supervised learning is particularly effective in environments where historical data with known outcomes is available. For instance, a supervised approach could be employed in a scenario where past incidents of security breaches are clearly documented, enabling the model to learn the characteristics of successful attacks. This can prove essential in automated threat detection systems that require high accuracy to reduce false positives. On the other hand, when it comes to discovering previously unknown threats or unusual patterns that don't conform to existing models, unsupervised learning methods come to the forefront. A real-world application might involve monitoring network behaviour over time to identify abnormal spikes in traffic that could signify denial-of-service attacks. Understanding the strengths and limitations of these models helps cybersecurity professionals strategically deploy AI technologies within their network architecture effectively, maximizing security while minimizing disruption.

When considering the implementation of machine learning models, keep in mind that data quality and quantity are crucial for achieving reliable outcomes. Regularly updating training datasets with the latest cybersecurity incidents can help ensure the sustained effectiveness of supervised models, while robust pre-processing steps can enhance the detection capabilities of unsupervised models. Incorporating explainability and interpretability into these models can also aid security teams in understanding AI decisions, fostering trust and enabling more informed responses to potential threats.

5.2 Training AI Models with Security Data

Acquiring and preparing security data for training AI models is a critical step in developing effective cybersecurity solutions. Security data should be diverse and representative of the various scenarios the AI model will encounter. This includes gathering data from multiple sources such as intrusion detection systems, firewall logs, user behaviour analytics, and threat intelligence feeds. It is essential to ensure that the data is both comprehensive and relevant, allowing the AI model to learn effectively. Data cleaning is another vital aspect of preparation.

This involves removing duplicates, addressing missing values, and ensuring that the data formats are consistent. Additionally, considering the data's context is critical; for example, understanding the environmental factors that could affect the data can lead to more accurate interpretations during training. By implementing best practices for data acquisition and cleaning, cybersecurity architects can significantly enhance the quality of the training data, leading to better outcomes from AI models.

Data labelling and feature selection are crucial components that directly influence the training process of AI models. Accurate data labelling ensures that the AI can learn from the right examples. For instance, classifying network traffic as benign or malicious enables the model to differentiate between normal behaviour and potential threats. Effective labelling requires expertise in cybersecurity, as it involves identifying not only the obvious threats but also nuanced patterns that an AI might miss without proper guidance. Feature selection, on the other hand, is the process of identifying and selecting the most relevant attributes from the data that will improve the model's performance. In cybersecurity, this could mean determining which user behaviours, network traffic patterns, or system logs provide the most insight into identifying an attack. Selecting the right features reduces the complexity of the model, enhances its processing speed, and improves its accuracy. Thus, prioritizing data labelling and feature selection can significantly enhance the model's ability to predict and respond to security incidents effectively.

To maximize the effectiveness of AI in cybersecurity, professionals should continuously iterate on the training process. Regularly updating the training dataset to include new and emerging threats ensures that the model adapts to the ever-evolving landscape of cybersecurity risks. It is equally important to evaluate the model's performance regularly and adjust the training parameters based on real-world feedback. Having a dynamic training process allows for the integration of new insights and knowledge into the model, fostering an adaptive security posture. Engaging in collaborative efforts with cybersecurity professionals to share data and insights can provide additional context that enhances training efficiency and effectiveness. A practical approach here is to create a feedback loop with continuous monitoring, keeping the AI models aligned with the latest threat intelligence and attack vectors.

5.3 Evaluating Model Performance

Defining metrics and benchmarks is a crucial step in assessing the performance of security-related AI models. Metrics such as accuracy, precision, recall, and F1 score provide a foundational understanding of how well a model performs in identifying threats and anomalies. Accurate detection of threats is essential, as false positives can lead to unnecessary resource expenditure while false negatives may leave systems vulnerable. In the context of cybersecurity, a balanced approach to these metrics ensures that models are finely tuned to mitigate risks effectively. Benchmarks can take the form of industry standards, historical data, or comparative analyses against existing models. Establishing clear benchmarks allows organizations to set realistic performance expectations and gauge improvements over time, aligning model performance with strategic security objectives.

Exploring tools and methodologies for ongoing model evaluation and refinement is vital for maintaining the effectiveness of AI in security applications. Continuous evaluation ensures that AI models adapt to evolving threat landscapes, which is crucial as cyber threats are dynamic and increasingly sophisticated. Automated monitoring tools can facilitate the real-time assessment of model performance, providing insights into metrics over time and revealing areas for improvement. Techniques such as cross-validation and A/B testing can be valuable in comparing different models or configurations, allowing teams to make data-driven decisions. Regularly updating training datasets to include new threats or behavioural patterns further enhances a model's relevance. Employing these tools allows cyber security professionals to maintain high standards in their defenses, ensuring that AI implementations remain robust and responsive to new challenges.

Practical monitoring strategies, including setting thresholds for alerts based on model predictions, can help in catching potential issues early on. Regularly revisiting the chosen metrics to align them with business goals ensures that model performance remains focused on the most relevant security concerns. By fostering a culture of continuous improvement and leveraging advanced tools, organizations can stay one step ahead in the battle against cyber threats.

Chapter 6: The Dark Side of AI

6.1 AI-Driven Cyber Attacks

Recent developments in artificial intelligence (AI) are dramatically reshaping the landscape of cyber threats. A prominent area of concern is the rise of AI-driven cyber attacks, which are becoming increasingly sophisticated and capable of automated exploitation. Phishing tactics have evolved beyond simple deceptive emails, leveraging AI to personalize and target victims with greater precision. These attacks can analyze social media profiles and other publicly available data to craft messages that appear authentic, greatly increasing the likelihood of success. Automated exploitation tools utilize machine learning algorithms to scan for vulnerabilities in software and systems at unprecedented speeds. By quickly identifying weaknesses, these tools can execute attacks before organizations even realize they are under threat, making traditional defense mechanisms less effective. As the AI ecosystem constantly evolves, cyber attackers are empowered with tools that can learn and adapt, making the need for advanced security solutions ever more pressing.

The potential impact of AI-driven cyber attacks on organizational security cannot be overstated. These attacks can compromise sensitive data, disrupt operations, and cause significant reputational damage. The automation and efficiency afforded by AI allow attackers to target multiple organizations simultaneously, which can overwhelm security teams and lead to a higher chance of successful breaches. Furthermore, the ability for AI to continuously learn from previous attacks means that cyber threats are becoming more persistent and difficult to predict. Organizations without robust AI-enhanced security measures may find themselves at a substantial disadvantage, as they struggle to respond to threats that evolve in real time. The implications extend beyond immediate financial losses; they can also affect customer trust and compliance with regulatory requirements, leading to long-term consequences for businesses.

Adapting to the landscape of AI-driven threats requires foresight and strategic planning from cybersecurity professionals. It is essential to integrate AI technologies into security architecture, enhancing threat detection and response capabilities. Incorporating machine learning algorithms can help identify patterns of malicious behaviour, fortifying defenses against evolving attacks. Additionally, investing in continuous training and awareness programs for employees can mitigate the risks associated with phishing and social engineering techniques, which remain prevalent despite technological advancements. Understanding the capabilities and limitations of AI in the context of cybersecurity is crucial for building resilient systems that can withstand increasingly sophisticated threats.

6.2 Manipulation of AI for Malicious Purposes

Malicious actors can manipulate AI systems for personal gain in numerous ways, with data poisoning being a significant method that compromises the integrity and functionality of AI technologies. Data poisoning occurs when adversaries deliberately corrupt the data used to train AI models, leading to inaccurate predictions or classifications. By introducing misleading or harmful data into the training sets, these actors can manipulate the AI's learning process. This form of attack is especially dangerous because it often goes unnoticed until the system behaves unexpectedly or causes harm. Examples include altering datasets that are designed to improve image recognition, which could lead AI systems to misidentify objects or people in critical scenarios. Such vulnerabilities not only undermine the performance of AI systems but can also lead organizations to make flawed decisions based on unreliable outputs, further increasing the risk of security breaches.

Several case studies underscore how malicious actors exploit these vulnerabilities within AI technologies. One notable instance is the attack on a facial recognition system where an attacker introduced a series of masked faces into the training dataset. This alteration resulted in the AI failing to recognize individuals in a variety of legitimate scenarios, demonstrating that a well-executed data poisoning scheme can significantly impair a system's effectiveness. Similarly, in the world of autonomous vehicles, attackers have shown that they can modify road sign appearances in such a way that the AI misinterprets their meanings, leading to potentially catastrophic consequences. The consequences of these exploitation tactics highlight not only the need for robust AI training protocols but also a comprehensive understanding among cybersecurity professionals about how to defend against such manipulative attacks.

When considering the implications of AI in network planning and security, it is crucial for professionals in the field to approach the integration of AI with a vigilant mindset. Implementing layered security strategies that include constant monitoring and evaluation of data inputs can help safeguard against the manipulation of AI systems. As malicious techniques evolve, so too must the methodologies for protecting AI assets. Establishing a culture of security-first thinking within organizations can significantly mitigate the risks associated with AI vulnerabilities, ensuring that these powerful technologies can be used securely and effectively.

6.3 Case Studies of AI Exploits

Throughout the past few years, various sectors have faced notable case studies of artificial intelligence (AI) exploits, demonstrating both the capabilities and vulnerabilities of AI systems. One such case occurred in the healthcare sector, where an AI-driven diagnostic tool was hacked to produce false positive results for certain medical conditions. This breach not only put patient safety at risk but also highlighted the dire consequences AI relies on the integrity and security of its input data. In another instance, an AI model used in the financial sector was manipulated to generate fraudulent credit scores, leading to significant monetary losses for several lending institutions. These cases underscore the critical intersection between advanced technologies and the malicious tactics employed by cyber adversaries. Exploits of AI systems can lead to widespread distrust, damage to reputations, and regulatory scrutiny, making them a pressing concern for cybersecurity professionals.

Evaluating these case studies reveals vital lessons that can better inform security practices. First, thorough security assessments should be integrated during the development of AI applications. This includes rigorous testing phases and real-time monitoring systems to identify and mitigate vulnerabilities proactively. Organizations should establish comprehensive guidelines that incorporate ethical considerations and data integrity into AI system design. Additionally, interdisciplinary collaboration is essential, bringing together AI developers, cybersecurity experts, and organizational leaders to design and implement robust security frameworks. Training personnel to recognize and respond to potential AI threats is another critical step. Constant vigilance and proactive threat modelling can create a security culture that anticipates rather than reacts to vulnerabilities. Adopting robust encryption methods and continuous threat assessments will also aid in protecting AI infrastructure from burgeoning cyber threats.

Staying informed of the evolving threat landscape is crucial for cybersecurity architects and engineers aiming to leverage AI in network planning, architecture, and security. Continually analyzing emerging vulnerabilities associated with AI will allow professionals to adapt their strategies accordingly. Engaging in ongoing education about AI advancements and potential exploits can serve as a proactive measure against current and future threats. As AI continues to permeate various sectors, the importance of embedding security into its architecture cannot be overstated. By prioritizing security integration at every stage of AI development, organizations can mitigate risks and harness the potential of AI responsibly.

Chapter 7: Ethical Considerations in AI Deployment

7.1 Ethical Dilemmas in Cyber Security

Integrating AI into cybersecurity protocols presents several key ethical dilemmas that cyber security professionals must grapple with. One of the foremost concerns centres around the transparency and explainability of AI-driven decisions. When artificial intelligence systems make critical decisions—such as identifying a potential threat or determining access permissions—understanding the rationale behind those decisions can be challenging. This lack of clarity complicates accountability, making it difficult to determine who is responsible when something goes awry. Additionally, there is a risk of entrenched biases within AI algorithms, which may lead to discriminatory practices. If these systems are trained on flawed data, they can perpetuate existing biases, leading to unfair treatment of individuals based on race, gender, or other sensitive characteristics. This raises significant ethical questions about the fairness and integrity of AI systems, especially when they are deployed to combat cyber threats.

Examining the societal implications of AI decisions within the security domain further highlights the importance of ethical considerations. The deployment of AI technologies in cybersecurity can lead to widespread surveillance, raising privacy concerns among individuals and communities. As AI systems monitor network activity and user behaviour to identify anomalies, the potential for misuse of data increases. This could create situations where innocent individuals are unjustly monitored or flagged as threats based on erroneous AI outputs. Moreover, as AIs become more autonomous in their decision-making, there is a growing fear that they might make choices that prioritize organizational efficiency over individual rights. Cybersecurity professionals must recognize that their actions impact not just their organizations, but also the broader public. Implementing AI responsibly requires a commensurate sense of duty to society, ensuring that technologies are designed and used in ways that safeguard privacy and uphold ethical standards.

To navigate these ethical dilemmas effectively, cyber security architects and engineers need to prioritize transparency, accountability, and fairness in their AI systems. Engaging in ongoing discussions about ethics in technology and actively seeking input from diverse voices can help address biases and enhance the integrity of AI. Professionals should also routinely assess and audit AI decision-making processes to ensure they remain aligned with ethical standards and societal values, ultimately fostering trust between security systems and their users. Always remember that the goal is not merely to enhance security but to do so in a way that protects individual rights and benefits society as a whole.

7.2 Bias and Fairness in AI Algorithms

Fairness and bias considerations are critical components when developing artificial intelligence models, especially in the context of cyber security. AI algorithms are increasingly used to automate decision-making processes, which include threat detection, risk assessment, and incident response. Given that these models are trained on historical data, they can inadvertently learn and perpetuate existing biases present in that data. This phenomenon can lead to unfair treatment of certain groups, undermining the integrity of security measures. It is the responsibility of cyber security professionals to ensure that these models are inclusive, aiming for equitable outcomes that do not disproportionately affect any demographic. In planning and architecture, ethical AI implementation includes understanding the sources of bias and working diligently to mitigate them, ensuring a fair representation of all users in security frameworks. Ignoring these principles can negatively impact the engagement and trust of users who rely on these systems for protection.

The consequences of algorithmic bias extend beyond ethical concerns; they have real implications for security outcomes and public trust. When biases are unaddressed, they can result in significant security gaps that may be exploited by attackers, ultimately leading to vulnerabilities within a network. For instance, an AI system trained predominantly on data from one demographic might overlook risks or falsely identify threats from underrepresented groups. Such inaccuracies not only weaken the effectiveness of security responses but can also lead to unwarranted scrutiny of specific populations, breeding mistrust in the technologies employed. The fallout from these biases can tarnish the reputation of organizations, putting them at risk of regulatory scrutiny, public backlash, and financial loss while diminishing trust in AI as a reliable tool for safeguarding critical infrastructure. Cyber security professionals need to recognize that the reliability of AI is intrinsically linked to the fairness of the data and algorithms that drive it.

7.3 Regulatory Compliance for AI in Cyber Security

In the rapidly evolving domain of cybersecurity, the integration of artificial intelligence presents unique challenges and opportunities. Numerous regulations impact the use of AI in this space, and organizations must navigate them carefully to avoid potential pitfalls. Key regulations such as the General Data Protection Regulation (GDPR) in Europe establish stringent guidelines concerning data protection and privacy, even when using AI technologies. It mandates that organizations ensure data subjects are informed about how their data is processed, which becomes increasingly complex with AI's inherent opaque decision-making processes. Similarly, in the United States, frameworks like the Federal Information Security Management Act (FISMA) and the Cybersecurity Framework by the National Institute of Standards and Technology (NIST) emphasize risk management and security controls that must be manually adapted for AI systems. Overall, understanding these regulations is critical, as failure to comply can result in hefty fines or reputational damage, hampering an organization's ability to leverage the advantages AI offers in the fight against cyber threats.

Ensuring compliance when deploying AI systems in cybersecurity requires adherence to best practices, which must be embraced throughout the entire lifecycle of the technology. Organizations should begin with data governance, ensuring that data is collected, processed, and stored in ways that are ethical and lawful. Establishing a multi-disciplinary team that includes legal, technical, and compliance experts can bridge the gap between regulatory requirements and AI development. Regular audits and assessments play a vital role in keeping AI systems aligned with compliance mandates, as they allow organizations to frequently evaluate risks associated with algorithm biases or data integrity issues. Furthermore, transparency in AI algorithms is critical; adopting explainable AI techniques can help demystify decision processes and make it easier for compliance teams to validate that the AI operates within acceptable ethical boundaries.

Integrating AI into cybersecurity strategies not only demands compliance with regulations but also necessitates a proactive approach to risk management. Organizations should implement iterative testing and updating of AI models in accordance with changing regulatory landscapes and emerging threats. Regular training sessions for staff on compliance and ethical considerations related to AI in cybersecurity reinforce a culture of security awareness. Additionally, leveraging tools that monitor adherence to regulatory standards and track changes in applicable laws can streamline the compliance process. By establishing a robust framework for compliance while embracing AI's transformative potential, organizations can effectively enhance their cybersecurity posture and respond to challenges with agility.

Chapter 8: AI for Incident Response

8.1 Automating Incident Detection

Artificial Intelligence (AI) significantly enhances the speed and efficiency of incident detection processes. In traditional cybersecurity frameworks, detection often relies on predefined rules and signatures that can be slow to adapt to new threats. AI, particularly machine learning, brings the ability to analyze large volumes of network traffic and user behaviour in real-time, enabling quicker identification of anomalies that could indicate a security incident. By employing advanced algorithms, AI can discern between normal and abnormal patterns far more rapidly than human analysts, which not only reduces the time to detect potential threats but also lowers the chances of human error. This leads to a more proactive security posture where incidents can be addressed as they emerge, minimizing their impact on organizational operations.

Integration frameworks that utilize machine learning for real-time alerts present a cohesive approach to enhancing incident detection capabilities. These frameworks allow cybersecurity systems to work in tandem with AI tools that continuously learn from the environment they monitor. By incorporating diverse data sources—such as logs from different systems, users' behavioural patterns, and external threat intelligence—these integrated solutions can generate alerts based on a holistic view of the organization's security landscape. This ensures that alerts are not just reactive but also contextual, providing security teams with actionable insights to prioritize their response efforts swiftly. Furthermore, establishing this synergy between various technologies and machine learning models facilitates the automation of mundane tasks, allowing cybersecurity professionals to focus on higher-level strategic initiatives that require their expertise.

Organizations looking to implement AI-driven incident detection should consider the importance of continuous learning in their models. Machine learning systems improve over time by training on new data, so it is crucial to regularly update the models with relevant incident data and threat intelligence. Additionally, fostering a culture of open communication between AI systems and cybersecurity teams can enhance the effectiveness of this technology, as human insights can help refine algorithms and highlight areas that require additional focus. Ultimately, starting with a pilot project can provide valuable learning opportunities and pave the way for broader application of AI in incident detection across the network.

8.2 AI in Incident Analysis and Recovery

Utilizing AI tools offers significant advantages in identifying the root cause and extent of security incidents. By leveraging machine learning algorithms and advanced analytics, organizations can examine vast amounts of data in real time. These AI systems can detect anomalies and patterns that may elude human investigators, allowing for a more precise identification of vulnerabilities and threats. For instance, AI can assess logs from various network devices, user activities, and transaction records to pinpoint unusual behaviours that signal a security breach. This process reduces the time typically taken to investigate incidents, streamlining the approach to incident response and minimizing potential damage.

Recovery strategies that integrate AI technology can enhance the overall incident response framework. One powerful application of AI in recovery is its capability to automate response actions based on predefined security policies. This means that when an incident is detected, AI can initiate containment measures, such as isolating affected systems or blocking malicious IP addresses, without human intervention. Furthermore, AI can play a critical role in post-incident recovery by analyzing the incident data to evaluate the effectiveness of the response actions taken, identifying areas for improvement. Machine learning can also help predict future incidents by recognizing trends from past incidents, enabling proactive defenses and reduced recovery times.

Implementing AI in incident analysis and recovery not only accelerates the response rate but also improves the accuracy and effectiveness of the actions taken. Cybersecurity professionals should consider integrating AI solutions within their existing security infrastructure to enhance their incident detection and recovery capabilities. By continuously refining these strategies and utilizing insights drawn from AI analysis, organizations can build a resilient security posture capable of adapting to evolving threats. It is advisable to keep abreast of the latest AI developments and explore pilot projects to evaluate their applicability within specific network environments.

8.3 Lessons Learned and Continuous Improvement

Learning from past incidents is crucial for enhancing artificial intelligence models and refining incident response strategies. Each cyber incident serves as a case study from which important lessons can be extracted. By analyzing how AI systems reacted during these events, cybersecurity professionals can identify weaknesses in their predictive algorithms and response protocols. Understanding the shortcomings that emerged in real-time situations allows engineers to adjust their models, incorporating feedback loops that strengthen AI decision-making processes. This iterative learning process not only improves the models but also enhances the overall resilience of the cybersecurity architecture, making systems more adaptive to evolving threats.

Implementing frameworks for continuous improvement in the AI incident management process is essential for staying ahead of adversaries. Several established methodologies can be adapted for this purpose, such as the Plan-Do-Check-Act (PDCA) cycle and Lean Six Sigma principles. These approaches facilitate regular assessment and optimization of both technologies and processes. By systematically evaluating performance, teams can identify bottlenecks and ineffective practices, enabling them to re-engineer workflows that incorporate AI insights more effectively. Assessing incident response through simulations can also help to reveal gaps in existing strategies, allowing organizations to refine their approaches before actual incidents occur. This proactive stance ensures that learning is not just reactive but becomes an integral part of the organization's culture.

Maintaining a focus on continuous learning provides tangible benefits. Regularly updating AI models with new data gathered from past incidents ensures that system responses are based on the most current threat landscape. Leveraging advanced analytics can provide deeper insights into patterns of behaviour that precede incidents, thus equipping security teams with tools to predict and mitigate potentially damaging events. By fostering a proactive learning environment and integrating feedback mechanisms into daily operations, cybersecurity professionals can enhance both the effectiveness of AI applications and their incident management strategies, making their networks more secure and resilient against future threats.

Chapter 9: Future Trends in AI and Cyber Security

9.1 Evolution of AI Technologies

Recent advancements in artificial intelligence technologies are significantly reshaping the cybersecurity landscape. Machine learning and deep learning algorithms are becoming increasingly sophisticated, enabling them to analyze vast amounts of data in real-time. This capability allows for the detection of unusual patterns or anomalies that could signify a cyber threat. For instance, AI-driven systems can identify potential vulnerabilities before they are exploited by malicious actors, providing organizations with the tools to enhance their proactive security measures. Natural language processing (NLP) has also emerged as a crucial aspect of cybersecurity, as it enables systems to understand and respond to human language, thereby enhancing threat intelligence analysis and incident response. Furthermore, AI is being integrated into security operations centres (SOCs), where it can assist analysts in triaging alerts and prioritizing responses based on the severity of threats.

Emerging technologies, particularly quantum computing, hold the potential to dramatically impact AI in the field of security. Quantum computing offers unparalleled computational power, which could enhance AI's capabilities in processing and analyzing data at a scale previously unimaginable. However, it also poses specific risks, especially in the realm of encryption. As quantum computers become more powerful, traditional encryption methods may be rendered obsolete, necessitating a re-evaluation of security protocols. AI can play a crucial role in developing quantum-resistant algorithms that will secure networks against future threats. Cybersecurity professionals must remain vigilant and start integrating quantum-safe strategies into their AI frameworks, ensuring that as AI technologies evolve, they are also equipped to withstand the challenges posed by the quantum era.

Understanding the interplay between AI advancements and quantum computing is essential for cybersecurity professionals. Staying informed and integrating innovative security measures will be key in navigating this evolving landscape. As AI technologies progress, continuous adaptation and exploration of AI-driven solutions will enable organizations to enhance their security posture, reducing vulnerabilities and increasing their resilience against evolving threats.

9.2 Predicting Future Threat Landscapes

As artificial intelligence continues to advance, the landscape of cyber threats is poised to evolve significantly. One key trend involves the utilization of AI by malicious actors to enhance their attack strategies. This could manifest in increasingly sophisticated phishing attacks, where AI generates credible-looking emails or messages that are tailored to specific individuals based on their online behaviour. Furthermore, AI algorithms can be leveraged to automate the discovery of vulnerabilities within systems, enabling attackers to find and exploit weaknesses much more rapidly than ever before. Additionally, we can anticipate the rise of deepfake technology, which may be used to impersonate executives or key personnel within organizations, potentially leading to significant security breaches via social engineering tactics.

To prepare defenses against these emerging threats, organizations should adopt a proactive and multifaceted approach. Implementing AI-based security solutions can enhance threat detection and quick response capabilities, allowing cybersecurity teams to identify unusual patterns indicative of an attack. Continuous monitoring and analysis of network traffic, combined with machine learning models, can help organizations stay one step ahead of attackers by recognizing anomalies that traditional systems might miss. Furthermore, regular training and awareness programs will be crucial in educating employees about the evolving nature of cyber threats, empowering them to recognize and report suspicious activities swiftly. Having a robust incident response plan that is regularly updated to reflect new threats is also essential in mitigating the impact of a successful attack.

Investing in ongoing research and collaboration within the cybersecurity community can provide valuable insights into emerging threats and defense mechanisms. By fostering partnerships and sharing knowledge on best practices, organizations can better anticipate and prepare for the challenges that AI-driven attacks present. Emphasizing a culture of innovation within security teams, paired with the continuous evolution of security protocols, will be key as we navigate an increasingly complex threat landscape powered by artificial intelligence.

9.3 Preparing for Emerging Technologies

Organizations must embrace proactive strategies to counter the rising tide of AI-driven security threats. This begins with fostering a culture of continuous learning and adaptation among security teams. Cybersecurity professionals should regularly engage in training sessions and simulations that incorporate AI scenarios, thereby sharpening their skills to detect and respond to AI-enhanced threats. Implementing advanced threat hunting and intelligence-driven security operations allows organizations to pre-emptively identify potential vulnerabilities and unusual behaviour patterns before they escalate into security breaches. Furthermore, exploring machine learning algorithms to analyze large datasets can help organizations predict and adapt to new threat vectors, significantly strengthening their defenses.

Collaboration is pivotal in the ever-evolving field of cybersecurity. AI technology developers and cybersecurity experts can mutually benefit by sharing insights and strategies to enhance defenses against sophisticated attacks. By forging partnerships, organizations can leverage the specialized knowledge of AI developers to tailor security solutions that anticipate and mitigate risks unique to their infrastructure. Developing integrated teams that consist of both groups can lead to innovative security designs that not only react to threats but also evolve as new AI technologies emerge. This cross-disciplinary approach fosters a richer understanding of potential blind spots within security architectures, equipping professionals with the tools necessary to guard against threats before they materialize.

As AI technology continues to advance, it's crucial for cybersecurity professionals to stay informed of the latest trends and tools available. Regularly attending industry conferences, participating in workshops, and engaging in online forums can provide valuable insights into how AI can be effectively integrated into network planning and security infrastructure. Additionally, organizations should consider pilot projects to experiment with AI-driven security measures in a controlled environment. This hands-on experience will not only build familiarity with new technologies but also help identify their applicability and effectiveness within specific organizational contexts.

Chapter 10: Building a Security Architecture with AI

10.1 Defining Security Architecture Principles

Foundational principles that guide the development of AI-enhanced security architectures include the concepts of adaptability, robustness, transparency, and user-centric design. Adaptability ensures that security architectures can evolve in response to emerging threats and changes in the organization's risk landscape. Robustness focuses on building defenses that can withstand diverse attack vectors, maintaining protection even under stress. Transparency in AI systems results in understandable decision-making processes, allowing cybersecurity professionals to trust the automated recommendations made by these technologies. A user-centric design prioritizes the needs and behaviours of users, ensuring security measures do not hinder productivity while simultaneously securing sensitive data.

These foundational principles align closely with organizational goals and regulatory frameworks. For instance, organizations strive for resilience against cyber threats while ensuring compliance with legal standards. By adopting adaptable security architectures, organizations can meet evolving regulatory requirements efficiently. Transparency not only fosters trust among employees and stakeholders but also satisfies regulatory demands for explainability in automated systems, especially in sectors like finance and healthcare. The principle of user-centric design supports organizational objectives by enhancing user engagement and productivity while minimizing compliance risks, thereby creating a more secure and efficient work environment.

Incorporating these principles into the design and implementation of security architecture requires ongoing assessment and alignment with both internal strategies and external regulations. As AI technologies continue to evolve, cybersecurity professionals should continuously evaluate how these principles can be applied to enhance security measures effectively. This not only fortifies defenses but also builds a culture of security that integrates seamlessly into organizational workflows, ultimately resulting in a more resilient infrastructure.

10.2 Frameworks for Incorporating AI

Several architectural frameworks have emerged to facilitate the safe integration of AI into security practices. These frameworks are designed to manage the complexities associated with AI while ensuring that the core principles of security—confidentiality, integrity, and availability—are not compromised. One notable framework is the Cloud Security Alliance (CSA) Security, Trust & Assurance Registry (STAR), which provides a structured approach to assessing the security posture of cloud providers adopting AI technologies. Another important framework is the National Institute of Standards and Technology (NIST) Cybersecurity Framework, which helps organizations identify and manage cybersecurity risks associated with AI. This framework emphasizes the need for continuous monitoring, risk assessment, and security control enhancements tailored to AI-specific vulnerabilities. By leveraging these frameworks, cybersecurity professionals can systematically address challenges such as data privacy, model bias, and adversarial attacks, thus enabling a more secure integration of AI solutions into existing security protocols.

Specific use cases highlight the importance of adopting these frameworks within cyber defense strategies. For instance, organizations can implement AI-driven threat detection systems that analyze vast amounts of network data to identify and mitigate potential threats in real-time. Utilizing the NIST framework, cybersecurity teams can develop an AI protocol that includes machine learning models specifically trained to recognize patterns indicative of cyberattacks, thereby reducing the time to detect breaches. Additionally, the incorporation of AI in incident response can significantly streamline processes by automating response actions based on identified patterns, as outlined by the CSA framework. This automation not only enhances the speed and efficiency of responding to incidents but also allows human analysts to focus on more strategic decision-making. By understanding these frameworks and their applications, cybersecurity professionals can effectively align their AI initiatives with robust security practices, ensuring a resilient cyber defense posture.

Regularly revisiting and updating the frameworks in use is crucial as AI technologies evolve and new threats emerge. Continuous learning from AI implementations and their outcomes fosters improved strategies and security postures. Engaging in community discussions and collaborating with industry peers can provide invaluable insights to enhance the frameworks further. Consider documenting lessons learned during AI integration, as this can serve as a crucial resource for future projects and enable others in the field to avoid similar pitfalls. This iterative process of refinement will be key in harnessing AI's full potential in enhancing cybersecurity.

10.3 Best Practices for AI Implementation

Implementing AI technologies within existing security infrastructures requires a strategic approach to ensure smooth integration and effectiveness. First and foremost, organizations should conduct a thorough assessment of their current security measures and infrastructure. Understanding existing capabilities and identifying gaps will enable the effective alignment of AI tools with the organization's security objectives. It is also crucial to select AI technologies that complement and enhance existing systems. This means evaluating the interoperability of new AI solutions with legacy systems to prevent any disruptions that could arise from incompatibilities. Moreover, leveraging AI solutions that focus on automating routine security tasks can free up human resources for more complex problem-solving and strategic initiatives, ultimately leading to a more resilient security posture.

Training and resources are imperative for the effective implementation of AI in cybersecurity. Organizations must prioritize training sessions aimed at bridging knowledge gaps within teams about how AI technologies operate and their potential impact on security processes. This not only includes hands-on training for IT staff and security professionals but also extends to raising general awareness among all employees regarding AI's role in enhancing security protocols and practices. Additionally, establishing a culture of continuous learning is essential. Providing ongoing educational resources, such as access to online courses, workshops, and knowledge-sharing platforms, can empower cybersecurity professionals to stay updated with the latest advancements in AI technologies and practices. Investing in these resources can greatly enhance the efficacy of AI tools and ensure that they are wielded to their fullest potential. Focus on building a collaborative environment where teams can share insights and experiences related to AI deployments. Engaging in regular feedback cycles can help refine usage strategies and boost overall effectiveness.

Organizations that successfully implement AI also prioritize the establishment of clear metrics for success. These metrics should encompass both qualitative and quantitative aspects of security improvements resulting from AI technologies. Monitoring performance indicators regularly allows teams to evaluate the impact of AI deployments comprehensively and make informed adjustments where necessary. Therefore, having a robust feedback loop in the AI implementation process can enable organizations to pivot their strategies effectively and anticipate evolving threats. An important practical tip is to prototype AI solutions on a smaller scale before full deployment. This approach not only allows for testing and refinement but also helps in minimizing risks associated with large-scale implementation. By doing so, organizations can ensure that they effectively harness the power of AI to enhance their cybersecurity frameworks while being prepared to adapt to the complexities that may arise in the fast-paced landscape of cybersecurity.

Chapter 11: Risk Management and AI

11.1 Identifying Risks Associated with AI

The deployment of AI systems within cyber security introduces a range of unique risks that professionals in the field must understand and navigate. One prominent risk is algorithmic bias, where AI systems trained on biased data may perpetuate existing inequalities or make erroneous decisions, potentially undermining the integrity of security measures. Furthermore, adversarial attacks present a significant threat as they exploit the vulnerabilities in AI models, allowing cybercriminals to manipulate inputs to deceive the AI into making incorrect assessments or actions. Another area of concern is the opacity of AI decision-making processes; the complex nature of many AI algorithms can make it challenging for security architects to interpret and trust the conclusions drawn by these systems. This lack of transparency can lead to difficulties in accountability and compliance, particularly when AI systems are involved in sensitive decision-making processes such as threat detection. In addition to ethical concerns, AI systems also face the risk of technical failures. These failures can arise from software bugs, hardware malfunctions, or unforeseen interactions with other security technologies. A missed alert or a false positive resulting from such failures could have severe implications, emphasizing the need for rigorous testing and validation of AI-driven solutions. Understanding these risks is crucial for integrating AI into existing cyber security frameworks effectively.

To address the complexities surrounding the risks of AI technologies, several risk assessment frameworks have been developed specifically for AI applications. One widely recognized framework is the AI Risk Assessment Model, which emphasizes a systematic approach to evaluate potential threats, vulnerabilities, and the overall impact of AI systems within a cyber security context. This model encourages professionals to assess each component of an AI system, including data sources, algorithm integrity, and output interpretations, enabling a comprehensive view of the associated risks. Another valuable framework is based on the NIST Cybersecurity Framework, which has been adapted to incorporate AI-specific considerations. It provides a structured process for identifying risks, implementing security measures, and continuously monitoring AI system performance. These frameworks facilitate a broader understanding of risks and support informed decisions on when and how to integrate AI into network planning and architecture. Professionals can utilize these guidelines to conduct thorough risk assessments and prioritize mitigation strategies effectively, ensuring that AI technologies enhance rather than compromise an organization's security posture.

Incorporating these risk assessment strategies is critical not only for safeguarding AI systems but also for fostering trust among stakeholders and users. Cyber security professionals should actively engage in discussions about the ethical implications of AI technologies and strive for transparency in AI operations. As you assess your organization's readiness to adopt AI-driven solutions, consider implementing regular audits and fostering a culture of continuous improvement in AI security practices. This proactive approach will not only mitigate risks but also enhance overall security resilience and adaptability in an ever-evolving threat landscape.

11.2 Risk Mitigation Strategies

Identifying strategies for mitigating risks associated with AI misuse or failure requires an understanding of the unique challenges that AI technologies present. Organizations must first assess their AI implementations by identifying potential failure points and misuse scenarios. This involves analyzing data handling procedures, algorithmic decision-making pathways, and the interfaces through which users interact with AI systems. Employing strict access controls can prevent unauthorized users from tampering with AI models or data input processes. Additionally, incorporating transparency in AI algorithms can foster trust and provide clarity regarding how decisions are made, further reducing the chances of misuse. Regular training for staff on the proper use of AI systems enhances awareness of potential risks and promotes an organizational culture focused on cybersecurity vigilance. Utilizing explainable AI can also help stakeholders understand the underlying decision-making processes, enabling them to detect anomalies and potential misuses more effectively.

Continuous monitoring and auditing are critical components of effective risk management within AI infrastructures. It is essential to implement real-time oversight mechanisms that can flag unusual activities or deviations from expected behaviour. Utilizing advanced analytics tools to monitor performance metrics can help in identifying early warning signs of system failure or misuse. Regular audits complement these monitoring efforts by providing a framework for thorough reviews of AI systems against compliance standards and performance benchmarks. These audits should not only assess how well AI systems are functioning but also examine their decision impacts on users and stakeholders. Additionally, establishing a feedback loop where audit findings inform ongoing improvements in AI systems fosters an adaptive risk management approach. This proactive stance allows organizations to stay ahead of emerging threats and maintain the integrity of AI applications, ensuring that they contribute positively to network planning and security.

AI risk management is not a one-time effort; it requires continuous adaptation and adjustment to new threats and technologies. Organizations should consider establishing an ongoing risk assessment process that aligns with their broader cybersecurity strategies. This includes regularly updating training protocols for employees as AI technologies evolve, and ensuring that governance frameworks remain relevant and robust in light of technological advancements. Moreover, leveraging collaborative efforts with community forums and information-sharing platforms can enhance threat intelligence, thereby augmenting individual organizational capabilities with collective knowledge. Practical application of these strategies, such as integrating AI-driven anomaly detection systems, can also benefit continuous monitoring efforts while providing dynamic risk mitigation capabilities.

11.3 Assessing AI-related Vulnerabilities

Assessing the vulnerability of AI systems to threats and potential exploitation requires a systematic approach that combines traditional cybersecurity principles with unique considerations inherent to AI technologies. The complexity of these systems often obscures their vulnerabilities, making it challenging to identify potential attack vectors. One effective method is to conduct a thorough threat analysis, which involves identifying the assets at risk, understanding the possible adversaries, and evaluating the techniques employed to manipulate or exploit the system. This analysis should extend to examining the data that trains and feeds the AI models, as adversaries could introduce poisoned data to affect outcomes. Risk assessments should utilize methodologies like Common Vulnerability Scoring System

(CVSS) to rate vulnerabilities based on their severity and potential impact, integrating these scores into the overall risk management framework for the AI system.

Tools for vulnerability scanning and threat modelling are pivotal in this assessment process. Several sophisticated tools exist that can scrutinize AI algorithms for weaknesses, such as static analysis software that inspects code without executing it, as well as dynamic testing tools that evaluate system behaviour during operation. Moreover, automated machine learning tools can aid in uncovering hidden patterns indicating vulnerabilities that human analysts might overlook. In threat modelling, frameworks like STRIDE and PASTA can be employed to outline threats from various perspectives, assessing potential impact and the likelihood of exploitation. These frameworks guide professionals in identifying potential weaknesses in the AI system architecture and implementing appropriate security controls.

Incorporating a continuous monitoring strategy is essential, as the landscape of AI-related threats evolves rapidly. Engage in regular testing and validation of machine learning models to ensure they remain resistant to adversarial attacks over time. Additionally, consider developing a response plan that outlines procedures for scenarios involving AI exploitation, including potential recovery steps to safeguard data integrity and system functionality. By proactively assessing vulnerabilities and employing the right tools, cybersecurity professionals can bolster the resilience of AI technologies against emerging threats.

Chapter 12: Securing AI Systems

12.1 Security Challenges for AI Systems

AI systems face a myriad of security challenges that can significantly compromise their effectiveness and reliability. One of the most pressing issues is the vulnerability to adversarial attacks, where malicious actors manipulate input data to deceive AI models. This can occur in various contexts, such as image recognition or natural language processing, where subtle alterations can lead to drastic changes in output. For instance, adversarial images, which look normal to the human eye, can cause AI systems to misclassify objects. Moreover, the complexity of machine learning models often serves as a double-edged sword; while it allows for sophisticated predictions, it also creates a larger attack surface that adversaries can exploit. Another challenge is the opacity of many AI algorithms, particularly deep learning models. Their 'black box' nature makes it difficult for security teams to understand how decisions are made, which complicates the identification of weaknesses and potential exploits. Additionally, the reliance on large datasets not only poses a risk of data biases but also increases the likelihood of data poisoning, where attackers corrupt the training data to impact the model's behaviour.

The implications of these challenges for overall security architecture are profound. As organizations integrate AI into their network planning and security strategies, they must factor in these vulnerabilities from the outset. It is essential to implement robust security measures, including regular audits of AI systems, to monitor for signs of adversarial manipulation. Security professionals should adopt a layered defense approach, ensuring that AI systems are not only secure in their own right but also protected by broader network security protocols. For example, incorporating anomaly detection mechanisms can help identify unusual behaviour indicative of an attack. Furthermore, transparency in AI models can enhance security; investing in explainable AI techniques allows cybersecurity professionals to gain insights into how and why decisions are made, thus enabling better risk assessment and mitigation strategies. It is crucial for teams to engage in continuous learning, keeping abreast of the latest research in AI security to stay one step ahead of evolving threats.

Integrating AI into security frameworks offers immense potential but requires careful consideration of its unique vulnerabilities. By prioritizing security in the design and deployment phases and maintaining an adaptive security posture, organizations can harness the power of AI while mitigating associated risks effectively. One practical tip is to use techniques such as adversarial training in which models are exposed to adversarial examples during training to improve their resilience against such attacks. This proactive approach can significantly bolster the integrity and reliability of AI-driven security systems.

12.2 Protective Measures for AI Infrastructure

Organizations must adopt a multifaceted approach to secure AI systems against vulnerabilities, as these systems can often be targets due to their complexity and the sensitivity of the data they process. Implementing robust access controls is essential; this includes strict authentication processes to ensure that only authorized personnel can interact with the AI infrastructure. Role-based access controls help in limiting user permissions based on their professional needs, thus reducing the risk of unauthorized access. Furthermore, regularly updating the systems and applying patches can mitigate known vulnerabilities that threat actors may exploit. Monitoring and logging access to AI systems can also provide insightful data that helps in identifying suspicious activities and allows for fast response to potential breaches. Continuous assessment of the AI components through penetration testing and vulnerability scanning can keep the security posture proactive, enabling organizations to address potential risks before they are exploited. Developing an incident response plan specifically for AI incidents ensures that organizations are prepared to tackle threats and vulnerabilities promptly and effectively.

Best practices for securing AI implementations draw heavily on traditional cybersecurity principles, while also recognizing the unique challenges posed by AI technologies. For physical security, it is crucial to safeguard the hardware on which AI systems run. This includes utilizing locked server rooms and controlled access to critical systems, thereby preventing tampering or theft of resources. Network security measures are equally important. Employing firewalls, intrusion detection systems, and segmentation can help in isolating AI systems from general network traffic, minimizing exposure to potential threats. Additionally, using Virtual Private Networks (VPNs) for remote access ensures confidentiality and integrity of data in transit. On a software level, employing secure coding practices is vital when developing AI software to prevent common vulnerabilities, such as injection attacks. Regular security audits and code reviews help in maintaining the integrity of the codebase. Furthermore, integrating AI systems with existing security protocols allows for better monitoring and anomaly detection, enabling a responsive defense against evolving cyber threats.

To enhance the overall security posture of AI infrastructures, continuous education and training of personnel involved in AI systems is paramount. Cultivating a culture of security awareness and ensuring that team members understand potential threats fosters a proactive environment where knowledge can translate into action. Encouraging collaboration between cybersecurity and AI development teams promotes the sharing of insights and strategies for risk mitigation. Organizations should also remain vigilant about regulatory compliance as it pertains to data privacy and AI ethics, which not only safeguards against legal repercussions but also aligns the use of AI with broader organizational responsibilities. By integrating a systematic approach to vulnerability management with rigorous security practices across physical, network, and software layers, organizations can significantly enhance the resilience of their AI infrastructures against potential threats. Regularly updating security measures and re-evaluating strategies in light of new threats will keep organizations ahead of adversaries in this continually evolving landscape.

12.3 Monitoring and Auditing AI Utilization

Continuous monitoring and auditing of AI systems are vital for maintaining security compliance in any organization. As AI technologies become increasingly integrated into networks and operations, the potential risks and vulnerabilities associated with these systems also rise. It is essential for cybersecurity professionals to be vigilant in assessing how AI behaves in real-time, as any abnormalities may signal security breaches or ethical concerns. By establishing a robust monitoring framework, organizations can detect deviations from expected behaviour, ensure compliance with regulatory requirements, and safeguard sensitive data. Regular audits can help identify gaps in security protocols, verify the integrity of AI algorithms, and assess the operational effectiveness of AI systems. This proactive approach not only mitigates risks but also enhances the overall trustworthiness of AI solutions, reassuring stakeholders that their data and operations are secure.

Effective oversight of AI systems requires the use of specialized tools and techniques suited for the unique characteristics of AI technologies. Traditional security tools may not be able to adequately analyze the complexity and scale of AI operations. Therefore, leveraging advanced monitoring solutions such as AI-driven analytics can provide insights into system performance and anomaly detection. Tools that incorporate machine learning algorithms can continuously learn from data patterns, allowing them to adapt to evolving threats and improving their detection capabilities over time. Additionally, utilizing automated auditing frameworks can streamline the process of evaluating compliance, generating reports that demonstrate adherence to security standards. These tools can help cybersecurity professionals to maintain an ongoing assessment of risk factors, review the decision-making processes of AI systems, and ensure accountability in AI utilization.

Ultimately, integrating continuous monitoring and rigorous auditing will not only strengthen an organization's security posture but also foster a culture of responsibility in AI utilization. Establishing comprehensive KPIs tailored for AI systems is crucial, as they can provide concrete metrics for evaluating effectiveness. Regular training and awareness programs for cybersecurity teams about AI's implications can further enhance active engagement with these technologies. Keeping abreast of evolving AI-related regulations and best practices will empower professionals to make informed decisions. Implementing a dynamic monitoring strategy tailored to the specific AI applications in use can significantly enhance network integrity, making it harder for adversaries to exploit any identified weaknesses.

Chapter 13: Collaboration between Cyber Security and AI

13.1 Interdisciplinary Approaches

The integration of artificial intelligence (AI) into cyber security represents a transformative shift in how organizations protect their systems and data. Interdisciplinary collaboration is paramount in this endeavour, as it brings together diverse expertise and perspectives from various fields. Cyber security is no longer the sole domain of specialists in network and information security; it intersects with machine learning, behavioural science, legal frameworks, and ethics. By fostering collaboration among professionals from these disciplines, organizations can enhance their AI-driven security strategies. For example, a cyber security architect can work alongside data scientists to develop machine learning models that identify anomalous behaviour indicative of cyber threats. Simultaneously, legal experts can ensure that these models comply with regulations governing data use and privacy, ultimately leading to more robust and effective security measures.

Effective practices for cross-domain partnerships among professionals are crucial for maximizing the potential of AI in cyber security. Creating platforms for regular communication between teams can facilitate the exchange of ideas and knowledge. Initiatives such as multidisciplinary workshops or joint projects encourage professionals from different domains to share their insights and develop innovative solutions collaboratively. Moreover, it is essential to establish a common language and understanding among these teams to mitigate any technical jargon barriers that might hinder collaboration. Utilizing collaborative tools that allow teams to visualize data and models can strengthen their joint efforts, making it easier to identify and tackle specific security challenges. Networking events and conferences dedicated to the intersection of AI and cyber security can also provide valuable opportunities for professionals to connect and build lasting partnerships focused on innovation and effectiveness in security architecture.

Integrating AI within cyber security is not merely a technological adoption; it's a collective journey that demands a synergy of expertise from various fields. Cultivating an interdisciplinary mindset ensures that AI applications are comprehensive, ethical, and aligned with broader organizational goals. As professionals engage in collaborative efforts, they should remain open to new ideas and perspectives, which will strengthen their impact on the security landscape. A practical tip for fostering such collaboration is to implement regular brainstorming sessions where team members from different backgrounds can present their challenges and collaborate on finding AI-enhanced solutions. This not only enriches the problem-solving process but also encourages continuous learning and adaptation in a rapidly evolving cyber threat environment.

13.2 Sharing Insights between Domains

Frameworks for sharing insights and data between AI researchers and cybersecurity practitioners are essential for bridging the gap between these two fields. The integration of artificial intelligence into cybersecurity practices relies heavily on both domains exchanging knowledge and datasets. AI researchers can provide algorithms designed to detect anomalies and predict threats, while cybersecurity practitioners bring domain-specific expertise and an understanding of the threat landscape. One effective approach to facilitate this exchange is the establishment of collaborative platforms or networks where experts from both fields can contribute their insights. These platforms can range from academic partnerships to industry consortiums, each designed to promote knowledge sharing, best practices, and collaborative tools. By developing standardized data sharing protocols and tools, stakeholders can ensure that both domains benefit from each other's strengths, improving the overall security framework.

Collaboration between AI researchers and cybersecurity professionals has the potential to significantly enhance security outcomes. By leveraging AI techniques, cybersecurity teams can automate threat detection and response processes, making them more efficient and effective. Machine learning models can analyze vast amounts of network traffic data to identify patterns and anomalies that human analysts may overlook. This not only speeds up the detection of security breaches but also reduces the workload on security teams, allowing them to focus on more complex issues. Additionally, AI can help in predictive analytics, which enables security professionals to anticipate potential threats and proactively strengthen defenses. This synergy can lead to a more proactive security posture, ultimately decreasing the number and impact of cyber incidents.

Understanding the timing and manner of integrating AI into network planning and security architecture is key for cybersecurity professionals. It is vital to assess the current security infrastructure and identify areas where AI can provide the most benefit, such as in threat detection, response automation, or improving user access controls. Regular feedback loops between AI systems and intelligence from cybersecurity operations can refine the AI's capabilities, leading to continuously improved security measures. By engaging in cross-domain dialogue and adapting AI solutions to meet specific security needs, organizations can foster a more resilient defense strategy.

13.3 Leveraging AI in Cyber Security Teams

Cyber security teams are increasingly recognizing that leveraging artificial intelligence tools can significantly enhance their operational efficiency. By integrating AI-driven technologies into daily workflows, these teams can automate mundane tasks, analyze vast datasets more swiftly, and detect anomalies that may elude human analysts. AI can streamline threat detection through machine learning algorithms that learn from historical data, flagging unusual patterns and potential breaches. Moreover, natural language processing can help in parsing through extensive logs and security alerts, prioritizing issues that require immediate attention. This not only optimizes resources but allows human experts to focus on more complex security challenges requiring nuanced thought and creativity.

Training strategies play a crucial role in ensuring that cyber security teams are proficient in utilizing AI-driven technologies. Comprehensive training programs should be established to educate staff on the fundamentals of AI and its specific applications within the security domain. Workshops that encompass hands-on experience with AI tools can significantly boost confidence and competence. Additionally, fostering a culture of continuous learning is essential, as AI technologies evolve rapidly. Regular simulations and role-playing scenarios can enhance team readiness, helping professionals understand how to respond to AI-generated alerts effectively. By investing in ongoing education and practical training, teams can cultivate a workforce that not only understands the technology but also knows how to leverage it for enhanced security outcomes.

To maximize the benefits of AI in cyber security, it's essential for teams to foster collaboration between AI experts and security analysts. This interdisciplinary approach can lead to the development of tailored AI solutions that align closely with the specific needs of the organization. Encouraging open communication about challenges and insights from both AI developers and security personnel can enhance the overall effectiveness of the AI tools in use. Keeping abreast of the latest advancements in AI technology will also ensure that cyber security teams remain agile and adaptive in an ever-evolving threat landscape.

Chapter 14: Training and Skill Development

14.1 Educational Needs for AI in Cyber Security

Cybersecurity professionals are increasingly required to understand artificial intelligence and its applications in network security. Key educational components necessary for professionals to thrive in AI-enhanced cybersecurity roles include a solid grasp of machine learning concepts, data analytics, and the ethical implications of AI. Familiarity with programming languages such as Python or R is also essential, as these languages are often used to build and deploy AI models. Furthermore, certifications in specific AI tools and platforms can greatly enhance a professional's skill set, ensuring they can effectively implement AI solutions within their organizations.

Emerging trends in curriculums and training programs are beginning to reflect the growing importance of AI in cybersecurity. Many universities and training organizations are integrating AI-focused modules into their existing cybersecurity programs, emphasizing hands-on experiences with real-world scenarios. Online learning platforms offer collaborative projects and labs that simulate AI applications in threat detection and response. Additionally, inter-disciplinary programs that bridge AI, cybersecurity, and data science are gaining traction, providing a comprehensive skill set that meets the demands of modern security challenges. To prepare effectively for these roles, professionals should seek out educational opportunities that emphasize continuous learning and adaptation to technological advancements.

As a practical tip, engaging in community forums and attending workshops can provide insights into the latest AI tools in cybersecurity. Staying updated on research developments and participating in relevant discussions can enhance one's understanding and inform strategic decisions in network planning and architecture.

14.2 Training Programs and Resources

Numerous training programs and resources are available for cybersecurity professionals who wish to specialize in artificial intelligence (AI). Institutions such as SANS Institute, Coursera, and edX offer a variety of courses specifically tailored to the intersection of AI and cybersecurity. SANS Institute provides immersive boot camps focused on topics like threat intelligence and data analysis, emphasizing how AI can enhance threat detection and response. Meanwhile, platforms like Coursera feature comprehensive courses from renowned universities that cover machine learning basics and AI applications in cybersecurity. These platforms also frequently update their content, ensuring that learners are exposed to the latest advancements and tools in the field.

Another noteworthy resource is the Artificial Intelligence Cyber Security Certificate offered by various universities. This program typically covers not only foundational AI principles but also ethical considerations and implications of using AI in security. Additionally, organizations such as the International Association of Privacy Professionals (IAPP) provide specialized training focused on the privacy aspects of AI and its role in cybersecurity. By participating in these training programs, professionals not only gain knowledge but also valuable certifications that can bolster their credentials in a rapidly evolving job market.

The trends in online learning and certification relevant to AI in cybersecurity indicate a growing shift toward digital platforms, driven by the need for flexibility and accessibility. The global pandemic accelerated the adoption of remote learning, making it a standard practice for many professionals. Online programs now feature interactive elements such as forums, live discussions, and hands-on labs, enhancing the learning experience. Certifications from recognized bodies, such as Certified Information Systems Security Professional (CISSP) and Certified Ethical Hacker (CEH), are increasingly integrating AI components, ensuring that professionals remain relevant and market-ready. As organizations continue to embrace AI technologies for network planning, architecture, and security, being well-versed in these trends can help cybersecurity professionals strategically implement AI solutions effectively. Take advantage of these resources and trends by continuously updating your knowledge and skills, as this will empower you to make informed decisions in your organization's cybersecurity strategy.

14.3 Building a Skilled Workforce

Organizations today need to implement effective strategies to develop a workforce that is adept in both cybersecurity and artificial intelligence technologies. One essential approach is to foster a culture of continuous learning. By creating an environment that prioritizes education and encourages employees to pursue relevant certifications and training programs, organizations can ensure that their teams remain updated with the latest advancements in cybersecurity and AI. Offering workshops, lunch-and-learns, and access to online courses are practical ways to facilitate this continuous learning. Encouraging collaboration among departments can also lead to hybrid skill sets, where professionals share knowledge from their respective fields, enhancing the organization's overall capabilities in integrating AI into cybersecurity defenses.

Another strategy involves actively participating in industry events and conferences. This exposure not only enhances the visibility of the organization but also allows employees to engage with leading experts and learn about emerging trends and technologies. Additionally, establishing partnerships with educational institutions can be significant for creating internship and co-op programs, which provide students with real-world experience while simultaneously evaluating potential future employees. These initiatives not only build a pipeline of talent skilled in cybersecurity and AI but also foster relationships with the next generation of professionals.

Mentorship is an invaluable tool for career progression in cybersecurity and AI. Establishing formal mentorship programs within organizations can guide aspiring professionals, helping them navigate complexities in their fields. Pairing experienced cyber security architects and engineers with junior staff or interns fosters knowledge transfer and provides a supportive framework for professional growth. Mentorship can take various forms, including regular one-on-one meetings or project collaboration, which can enhance the learning experience further. Organizations should also consider creating clear pathways for career advancement. This could involve outlining skill requirements for different positions and encouraging employees to seek promotions based on demonstrated skills and accomplishments. A transparent career progression framework motivates employees by providing a clear vision of their professional journeys and encouraging them to acquire new skills, particularly in AI technologies that are increasingly integral to cybersecurity strategies.

To ensure a well-rounded skill set within the workforce, organizations can promote cross-functional training, enabling employees to understand the interdependencies between cybersecurity and AI. This multifaceted approach will not only strengthen individual capabilities but also enhance the overall security posture of the organization. Networking opportunities, both internally and externally, can also encourage professionals to connect and share insights, further promoting a culture of learning and collaboration. By investing in workforce development and fostering mentorship, organizations can create a skilled and adaptive workforce equipped to tackle the evolving challenges at the intersection of AI and cybersecurity.

Chapter 15: Conclusion and Future Outlook

15.1 Summarizing Key Insights

This book has delved into critical insights surrounding cybersecurity, emphasizing the multifaceted nature of threats and the necessity for adaptable frameworks. Throughout the chapters, we explored how evolving cyber threats have prompted a shift in cybersecurity strategies, highlighting the importance of risk assessment and proactive defense mechanisms. The implications of these insights stress that professionals within the cyber domain must embrace a continuous learning mindset and remain vigilant against emerging vulnerabilities. By adopting a layered security approach and integrating comprehensive threat intelligence, organizations can create robust cybersecurity frameworks that not only protect their assets but also support their overall mission. The landscape of cyber threats is ever-changing, and understanding the principles outlined in this book is fundamental to developing effective, forward-thinking security measures.

Looking ahead, artificial intelligence is set to play a pivotal role in shaping the future of cybersecurity. The infusion of AI in threat detection and response mechanisms offers tools that can analyze massive amounts of data at unparalleled speeds. This capability allows cybersecurity professionals to identify patterns and anomalies that may indicate an impending attack, enabling swift action to mitigate risks. Moreover, AI-driven systems can automate routine tasks, freeing up valuable time for engineers and architects to focus on strategic planning. As we continue to integrate AI into our cybersecurity frameworks, the need for collaboration between human expertise and machine learning will become crucial. Cybersecurity professionals must not only understand how to leverage AI technologies but also remain aware of their limitations and the ethical implications they introduce. Being proactive in developing these skills will ensure that we are well-prepared to harness AI's full potential in fortifying our networks and systems against ever-evolving threats.

As you move forward in your cybersecurity journey, consider embracing AI not just as a tool, but as a partner in your security architecture. Regularly evaluate and adapt your strategies based on the insights gained from AI-driven analysis. This dynamic approach will enhance your organizational resilience and preparedness in an environment defined by constant change and emerging threats.

15.2 Future Challenges and Opportunities

As artificial intelligence technologies continue to advance, the landscape of cybersecurity will experience significant challenges. One major concern is the growing sophistication of AI-powered cyber threats. Attackers may leverage machine learning algorithms to create highly adaptive malware capable of learning and evading detection mechanisms. This evolution makes it increasingly difficult for traditional security measures to keep pace, requiring cybersecurity professionals to adopt new strategies and technologies. Furthermore, the reliance on AI can lead to vulnerabilities in systems if the underlying algorithms are flawed or biased. These weaknesses can be exploited by malicious actors, posing serious risks to sensitive data and network integrity. Additionally, the ethical implications surrounding AI use in cybersecurity cannot be overlooked. The potential for misuse of AI technologies raises questions about accountability and trust, particularly in automated decision-making processes.

Despite these challenges, there are numerous opportunities for innovation within the field of cybersecurity. Artificial intelligence can enhance threat detection and response capabilities through the development of advanced analytics and real-time monitoring systems. These smart systems can analyze vast amounts of data at speeds unachievable by human operators, identifying patterns and anomalies that signify potential threats. Additionally, AI can automate repetitive tasks, allowing cybersecurity professionals to focus on more complex challenges. This can lead to increased efficiency and faster incident response times. Moreover, as organizations become more aware of the importance of cybersecurity, there is a surge in demand for AI-driven solutions tailored to specific industries, creating a fertile ground for cybersecurity engineers and architects to innovate and develop customized security architectures.

Recognizing the balance between challenges and opportunities is essential. Cybersecurity professionals should invest in learning and training related to AI applications to stay ahead of potential threats. Engaging in collaborative efforts with AI developers can also pave the way for creating more robust defense mechanisms. Establishing partnerships with academia and industry can enhance research and the practical application of AI technologies. By maximizing the opportunities presented by AI while addressing its associated challenges, cybersecurity professionals can create an adaptive and resilient security posture.

15.3 Final Thoughts on AI in Cyber Security

Bringing together the immense capabilities of artificial intelligence with the critical demands of cyber security presents both opportunities and challenges. As cyber threats evolve becoming increasingly sophisticated, the integration of AI offers a substantial advantage in threat detection, response times, and overall security architecture. However, this integration must be approached with a careful understanding of the inherent risks. The reliance on AI can introduce its vulnerabilities, ranging from algorithmic biases to potential exploitation by malicious actors who understand how to manipulate these systems. Cyber security professionals must remain vigilant, constantly assessing the balance between leveraging AI's power and managing these risks. Adopting AI should not mean abandoning traditional security measures but rather enhancing them to create a more robust defense mechanism. Continuous evaluation and adjustment will be essential as the technology and threats evolve.

Encouraging a proactive and forward-thinking mindset within the cyber security community is vital for successful AI implementation. Professionals should engage in ongoing training and education related to AI advancements to stay ahead of the curve. It's important to experiment with AI applications in controlled environments before full-scale deployments. Creating an iterative feedback loop where lessons learned from AI experiences can feed into future projects will foster a culture of innovation and resilience. Additionally, collaboration among stakeholders, sharing insights, and participating in professional networks will facilitate the effective integration of AI technologies. This collaborative spirit can drive the sustained improvements needed to enhance network security and build defenses that are not just reactive but anticipatory. To successfully incorporate AI, professionals should prioritize learning from both successes and failures while remaining adaptable to the ever-shifting threat landscape.

As a practical tip, focus on establishing a clear governance framework for AI deployments in cyber security. Define roles and responsibilities, set ethical guidelines for AI use, and ensure transparency in automated decision-making processes. This framework can help safeguard against the unintended consequences of AI, fostering a more secure environment as you harness its potential.

www.ingramcontent.com/pod-product-compliance
Lightning Source LLC
LaVergne TN
LVHW060124070326
832902LV00019B/3131